Benchmark ADVANCE

C0-APY-686

Fluency

Grade **3**

TABLE OF CONTENTS

About *Benchmark Advance* Intervention

Benchmark Advance Intervention is intended for students who need extra support to master grade-level standards. It offers reteaching and additional practice to reinforce instruction in the core program. *Benchmark Advance* Intervention provides direct instruction of the Reading Standards for Foundational Skills, Grades K–5, as outlined in the CA Common Core Standards. The standards are addressed as shown below.

Grade **K**	Grade **1**	Grade **2**	Grade **3**	Grades **4–6**
Print Concepts	**Print Concepts**	**Print Concepts**	**Print Concepts**	**Phonics and Word Recognition**
Phonological Awareness	**Phonological Awareness**	**Phonological Awareness**	**Phonological Awareness**	**Fluency**
Phonics and Word Recognition	**Phonics and Word Recognition**	**Phonics and Word Recognition**	**Phonics and Word Recognition**	
Fluency	**Fluency**	**Fluency**	**Fluency**	

At Grades K–3, individual grade-level packages of lessons and blackline masters address all of the reading foundation (RF) standards. An additional package for Grades 4–6 addresses the Phonics and Word Recognition and Fluency standards for Grades 2–5. In addition, each of the packages at Grades K–3 includes lessons and blackline masters to address the RF standards presented in previous grades. In this way, teachers can address the needs of students at each student's instructional level—whether at/near grade level or below.

The program offers skill-focused sequential and systematic instruction that is parallel to instruction in the core program. Each lesson is designed to target a specific skill that needs bolstering as revealed through program assessments.

It can be implemented flexibly in small groups or to individual students. Each lesson is designed to be completed in 15 minutes.

Lesson Structure

All of the fluency lessons in *Benchmark Advance* Intervention follow a consistent instructional design that offers explicit skills instruction and a gradual release model to scaffold student learning.

The side column at the start of every lesson furnishes the information teachers need to manage student learning:

- The target standard or standards that appear at the beginning of each lesson

- The prerequisite lesson(s) that should be completed before using the current lesson

- The specific Lesson Objective that states what students will be able to do after completing the lesson

- The Essential Question, which helps bring focus to the standard that is the focus of the lesson

- The Metacognitive Strategy, which increases awareness of the strategies students use as they learn

- The essential Academic Language and Additional Materials that students will use in the lesson

- A reminder of the prerequisite skills that students need to understand each lesson

The instructional lessons offer consistent and explicit instruction that helps students focus on the specific lesson objectives.

- The Introduce section and State Learning Goal set the learning goal for the lesson.

- The Before Read-Aloud or Before Reading section offers the opportunity to build background, activate prior knowledge, and make predictions.

- The During Read-Aloud or During Reading section includes teacher modeling, interactive reading, and echo-reading to build intonation and expression.

- The After Read-Aloud or After Reading section includes model questions for students to ask and answer, and retelling options to check comprehension.

- The Conclusion gives students an opportunity to restate what they've learned in the lesson.

- The Home Connection links the lesson to at-home practice within the family setting.

Every lesson ends with a point-of-use Formative Assessment so teachers can evaluate whether students have mastered the target skills. Intervention 2 suggestions provide alternative teaching ideas for working with students who need further support.

The blackline masters that accompany the lessons provide practice and application opportunities to promote standards mastery.

Corrective Feedback

Inherent in the teaching profession is the need to make corrections. In both structural and communicative approaches to language teaching and learning, feedback is viewed as a means of fostering learner motivation and ensuring linguistic accuracy (Ellis 2009). The purpose of the feedback is to close the gap between the student's current learning status and the lesson goals (Sadler 1989). Students can receive feedback in three ways: from their teacher, from peers, and through self-assessment.

Formative assessment is a process that teachers and students use during instruction. It provides feedback to inform ongoing teaching and learning approaches. Corrective feedback is also an essential feature of language development instruction. Teachers provide students with judiciously selected corrective feedback on language usage in ways that are transparent and meaningful to students. Overcorrection or arbitrary corrective feedback is avoided.

Corrective feedback is information given to learners regarding a linguistic error they have made (Loewen 2012; Sheen 2007). The feedback information can consist of any one or all of the following:

(a) **an indication that an error has been committed;**

(b) **provision of the correct target language form; or**

(c) **metalinguistic information about the nature of the error.**

Corrective feedback in the form of negotiating for meaning can help learners notice their errors and create meaningful connections, thus aiding acquisition. It is important to emphasize that language learners can only self-correct if they possess the necessary linguistic knowledge (Ellis 2003).

One solution sometimes advocated to this problem is to conduct corrective feedback as a two-stage process: first encourage self-correction and then, if that fails, provide the correction (Doughty and Varela 1998).

Corrective feedback can be:

Explicit
Explicit corrective feedback overtly draws the learner's attention to the error made.

Implicit
Implicit corrective feedback focuses the learner's attention without overtly informing the student that he/she has made an error or interrupting the flow of interaction.

Corrective Feedback Strategies

	IMPLICIT Attracts learner's attention without overtly informing the learner that he/she has made an error or interrupting the flow of interaction.	EXPLICIT Tries to overtly draw the learner's attention to the error made.
INPUT PROVIDING: **Correct form is given to students.**	**RECAST** The teacher incorporates the content words of the immediately preceding incorrect utterance and changes and corrects the utterance in some way (e.g., phonological, syntactic, morphological, or lexical). L: I went school. T: You went to school?	**EXPLICIT CORRECTION** The teacher indicates an error has been committed, identifies the error and provides the correction. L: We will go on May. T: Not *on* May, *in* May. T: We will go in May.
OUTPUT PROMPTING: **The student is prompted to self-correct**	**REPETITION** The teacher repeats the learner utterance highlighting the error by means of emphatic stress. L: I will showed you. T: I will *show* you. L: I will show you.	**METALINGUISTIC EXPLANATION** The teacher provides explanation for the errors that have been made. L: two duck T: Do you remember how to show more than one duck? L: ducks T: Yes, you remember that we need to add "s" at the end of a noun to show the plural form.
	CLARIFICATION REQUEST The teacher indicates that he/she has not understood what the learner said. L: on the it go T: Can you please tell me again? T: Do you mean "It goes on your desk"?	**ELICITATION** The teacher repeats part of the learner utterance but not the erroneous part and uses rising intonation to signal the learner should complete it. L: I don't think won't rain. T: I don't think it . . . (will) rain.
		PARALINGUISTIC SIGNAL The teacher uses a gesture or facial expression to indicate that the learner has made an error. L: Yesterday I go to the movies. T: (gestures with right forefinger over left shoulder to indicate past)

Adapted from: Ellis, Rod. "Corrective Feedback and Teacher Development." L2 Journal, volume 1 (2009).

Recommendations for English Learners

	Student Language and Literacy Characteristics	Considerations for Instruction
Oral Skills	**No or little spoken English proficiency**	**Students will need instruction in recognizing and distinguishing the sounds of English as compared or contrasted with sounds in their native language.** • The Center for the Improvement of Early Reading Achievement (CIERA) states that ELLs should learn to read initially in their first language. CIERA recommends that ELLs participate in read-alouds of big books, read along with proficient readers, and listen repeatedly to books read aloud in order to gain fluency in English (Hiebert et al. 1998). • Rhymes, poems, stories, and songs are present in most languages and cultures. The act of repeated listening to rhymes, poems, stories, and songs will help students become familiar and internalize the sounds and rhythm of the English language. • The particular language of rhymes, poems, stories, and songs will encourage and motivate English learners begin to produce both the familiar and unfamiliar sounds of the English language. • Visuals, gestures, emphasized rhythm, and varied voice intonation are used to convey and negotiate meaning.
	Oral skills: Spoken English proficiency	**Students will need instruction in applying their knowledge of the English sound system to foundational literacy learning.** • Rhymes, poems, stories, and songs provide English learners the opportunity to practice and build on the English language they already know. • The repetitive and playful language in rhymes, poems, and songs motivates English learners and helps them to feel confident and successful as they produce English fluently, with intonation and expression.
Print Skills	**No or little native language literacy**	**Students will need instruction in print concepts.** • Fluency practice includes basic print concepts such as tracking from left to right, return sweep, top to bottom, and page-by-page sequence. It also includes recognizing and naming all upper- and lowercase letters of the alphabet and understanding that letters represent sounds and, most important, that print carries a message.
	Some foundational literacy proficiency in a language not using the Latin alphabet (e.g., Arabic, Chinese, Korean, Russian)	**Students will be familiar with print concepts, and will need instruction in learning the Latin alphabet for English, as compared or contrasted with their native language writing system (e.g., direction of print, symbols representing whole words, syllables or phonemes).** • Beyond the directionality of print, and the relationship between phonemes and graphemes, engaging in meaningful repeated readings will help English learners gain familiarity with the Latin alphabet and the sounds it represents as well as building their foundational proficiency in English reading comprehension. • Using visuals, gestures, emphasized rhythm, and varied voice intonation and relating those specifically to words and phrases in the text will underscore that print, whether logographic or alphabetic, is the expression of thought and carries a message that can be voiced.
	Some foundational literacy proficiency in a language using the Latin alphabet (e.g., Spanish)	**Students will need instruction in applying their knowledge of print concepts, phonics and word recognition to the English writing system, as compared or contrasted with their native language alphabet (e.g., letters that are the same or different, or represent the same or different sounds) and native language vocabulary (e.g., cognates) and sentence structure (e.g., subject-verb-object vs. subject-object-verb word order).** • Familiarity with the Latin alphabet affords students the opportunity to avail themselves of their primary language skills to transfer their knowledge to English. • Repeated purposeful readings will enable students to construct meaning as they develop and produce the English language with fluency, intonation, and expression.

Please see the Contrastive Analysis Charts provided in the Teacher's Resource System.

Read Informational Text with Understanding, Intonation, and Expression RF.3.4a

CCSS RF.3.4
Read with sufficient accuracy and fluency to support comprehension.
a. Read on-level text with purpose and understanding.

Lesson Objectives

- Determine genre of text before reading and demonstrate understanding of the purpose for reading.
- Demonstrate an understanding of grade-appropriate vocabulary.
- Participate in guided/shared reading of different genres of text.
- Make and confirm predictions in text read aloud by the teacher.
- Read with intonation and expression.

Essential Question

How do readers know what kind of expression to use?

Metacognitive Strategy

Think while listening; plan, monitor, and evaluate listening; reference visuals and text features to predict and confirm understanding.

Academic Language

Informational text, topic, facts, details, explain, predict, sequence, first, next, then, last or finally

Additional Materials

- BLMs 7, 10, 19, 22, 31, 34, 43, 55, 58, Read for Understanding
- BLM 63, Self-Evaluation

Pre-Assess

Student's ability to listen with attention, understand what is being read aloud, and use text features

Student's understanding of how voice and expression are used to convey the meaning of text being read aloud

Introduce

- Students will be aware of a specific purpose for listening and reading.
- Students will demonstrate listening comprehension by responding to *wh-* questions or explaining what the text being read aloud is about.
- Students will demonstrate listening retention by explaining **facts** and **details**, using illustrations and text features, and by recalling words/phrases from the text.

State Learning Goal

Say: *Today we will read an* **informational text**. *The purpose for listening to the informational text will be to remember what it is about and to remember facts and details we found interesting. First, you will listen to the sound and tone of my voice as it changes when I read a text aloud.*

Ask: *What is the purpose for listening today? (To remember what the text is about, to listen to how your voice changes)*

Before Read-Aloud

Use the title and text features to establish the **topic** and activate prior knowledge. Build background knowledge by discussing illustrations, text language, and key vocabulary to make certain that students understand their meaning.

Ask: *What do you* **predict** *this text will be about? (Point out title, text features, and details in illustrations as clues to prediction.)*

During Read-Aloud

First Read: Model reading fluently at a natural pace, with intonation and expression, including emphasis on key facts or details, varying voice intonation to engage students and facilitate comprehension. Model reading without intonation, emphasis, or expression.

Ask: *Which reading did you like best? Why?*

Second Read: Interactive reading while thinking aloud, asking thoughtful questions, emphasizing key details, and confirming predictions.

- Ask and answer questions to demonstrate understanding of the text, referring to the text explicitly.
- Determine the main ideas. **Explain** how they are conveyed through key details.
- Describe the relationship in a text between a series of historical events, scientific ideas or concepts, or between steps in technical procedures, using language that highlights time, **sequence**, and cause/effect.

Third Read: Echo-read or choral-read with students, emphasizing appropriate pacing, intonation, and expression.

Say: *When we read aloud, the sound of our voice also gives meaning to the words.*

After Read-Aloud

Have students demonstrate understanding of text by asking them to retell the text in their own words, using key details and referencing illustrations. Support students by providing sentence starters as needed.

A topic is what the text is mostly about: The topic of this passage is _____.

A detail is information about the topic: One fact or detail the text provides is that _____.

Making connections to text: I learned that _____ is/are/can/ _____ and also that _____.

Conclusion

Ask: *What did we learn today?*

Say: *We learned that when we read, our voice and expression change along with the words. We read as we speak—not too quickly and not too slowly—so that we can understand what we read.*

Use the Self-Evaluation BLM (63) for student self-reflection, evaluation, and goal setting.

Home Connection

Ask students to take the informational text home to reread with a family member. Have students point out key details and events they remember and discuss with their family what the informational text is about.

✔ Formative Assessment

If the student completes each task correctly, proceed to the next skill in the sequence. If not, refer to suggested Intervention 2.

Did the student…?	Intervention 2
Recall the purpose for listening?	• Explain that a "purpose" is a "reason." Explain that we pay attention to what is read with a reason. *Say: We will listen to remember what the informational text is about We will remember key details and events.* (Provide examples.)
Connect to prior knowledge?	• Build new knowledge using illustrations, and provide personal examples that connect to what students already know.
Build understanding of vocabulary?	• Use visuals, quick sketches, gestures, and realia. Provide definitions and examples.
Predict what the informational text was about?	• Make connections between title, illustrations, and key vocabulary.
Recall key details and events?	• Reference informational text board illustrations and number events to correlate with illustrations. • Use an informational text structure graphic organizer to sketch and analyze informational text elements.
Echo-or choral-read?	• Echo-read one phrase or sentence at a time and check for understanding.
Retell informational text?	• Use an informational text board and sentence frames or sentence starters correlated to each picture.

CCSS: RF.3.4
Read with sufficient accuracy and fluency to support comprehension.
b. Read on-level prose and poetry orally with accuracy, appropriate rate, and expression on successive readings.

Prerequisite lesson: 1a

Lesson Objectives

- Listen to different genres being read aloud fluently.
- Read with accuracy, appropriate rate, and expression.
- Decode instructional-level words with increasing automaticity.
- Read sight words accurately and automatically.
- Use phrasing/fluency technique.

Essential Questions

How does grouping words help you read better? How does punctuation help a reader?

Metacognitive Strategy

Use selective attention and monitor comprehension while reading.

Academic Language

Pacing, fluency, words, phrases

Additional Materials

- BLMs, 8, 11, 20, 23, 32, 35, 44, 56, 59, Read for Expression
- BLM 63, Self-Evaluation

Pre-Assess

Student's ability to decode instructional-level words with automaticity and to understand text while reading it aloud

Read Informational Text with Accuracy, Appropriate Rate, and Expression RF.3.4b

Introduce

- Students will be aware of a specific purpose for reading.
- Students will read with proper phrasing and fluency.
- Students will demonstrate automaticity of instructional-level words.

State Learning Goal

Say: *Today we will read an* **informational text**. *The purpose for reading the informational text is to read with appropriate* **pacing** *and* **fluency**. *That means we will read not too quickly or too slowly, so that we can understand what we are reading. We will read* **words** *and* **phrases** *aloud so we can practice reading and understanding what we read.*

Ask: *What is the purpose for reading today? (I will read words and phrases aloud, so I can better understand what I read.)*

Before Reading

Explain that knowing when to pause and when to read words in a row without stepping can help students develop their understanding of a text. Tell students that they will practice pausing and reading words that go together naturally while reading an informational text.

During Reading

First Read: Teacher models reading each sentence with proper phrasing and fluency. Teacher reads the whole passage, pointing out punctuation marks. Then teacher rereads, asking students to listen to the changes in the tone of voice.

Second Read: Student reads each sentence progressively, scrolling down each line of the text.

Third Read: Student reads the whole informational text with appropriate fluency and pacing. Teacher monitors for student's accuracy, fluency, and pacing.

After Reading

Have students read to partners to demonstrate that they can use the sentence progression strategy to practice appropriate fluency and pacing.

Conclusion

Ask: *What did we learn today?*

Say: *We learned how to pause when reading, and how to read phrases that go together naturally. We read the same way we speak—not too quickly and not too slowly. We do this so that we can understand what we read. Punctuation helps readers know when to pause, stop, and change their tone of voice. Reading with appropriate pacing and intonation helps us understand what we read.*

Use the Self-Evaluation BLM (63) for student self-reflection, evaluation, and goal setting.

Home Connection

Ask students to take the informational text home to read with a family member. Have students practice the sentence progression strategy with members of their family.

✔ Formative Assessment

If the student completes each task correctly, proceed to the next skill in the sequence. If not, refer to suggested Intervention 2.

Did the student...?	Intervention 2
Recall the purpose for reading?	• Explain that a "purpose" is a "reason." Explain that we pay attention to how we read the text aloud so that it sounds like we are talking. This helps us understand what we are reading. *Say: We have to make sure that we are not reading too quickly or too slowly. We will read each word followed by the next until the words become a sentence that makes sense.*
Listen attentively while the teacher modeled?	• Model reading fluently while students echo-or choral-read. Conduct a cloze read as student chimes in with missing words.
Read each sentence progressively?	• Guide students in reading the words, phrases, and sentences by scrolling the text to expose one line at a time while it is being read.
Scroll from one line to another effortlessly?	• Have students practice tracking each word and using the return sweep with their finger as you read aloud together.
Read informational text with appropriate pacing?	• Guides students by tracking across the line of text while reading aloud together.
Read informational text with appropriate intonation?	• Select a portion of the text that requires varied intonation to practice reading. Discuss the meaning, feelings, and thoughts conveyed by the text—to explain why changing the tone of voice is necessary to express meaning and support understanding of the text.

CCSS: RF.3.4
Read with sufficient accuracy and fluency to support comprehension.
c. Use context to confirm or self-correct word recognition and understanding, rereading as necessary.

Prerequisite lessons: 1a, 1b

Lesson Objectives

- Read with purpose and understanding, determining whether or not the text is understood.
- Read with accuracy and comprehension, determining if a word is misread.
- Use context to determine meaning.
- Decode instructional-level words with increasing automaticity.

Essential Questions

What do I do when I do not know what a word means? What is an appropriate rate in reading?

Metacognitive Strategy

Use selective attention and monitor comprehension while reading; make inferences and use context clues.

Academic Language

Accuracy, comprehension

Additional Materials

- BLMs, 9, 12, 21, 24, 33, 36, 45, 57, 60, Recognize Words
- BLM 61, Recording Time Sheet
- BLM 62, Comprehension Monitoring
- BLM 63, Self-Evaluation

Pre-Assess

Student's ability to decode instructional-level words with automaticity and to understand text while reading it aloud

Read Informational Text to Confirm Word Recognition and Understanding RF.3.4c

Introduce

- Students will be aware of a specific purpose for reading.
- Students will read with accuracy and understanding, determining when they do not understand the meaning of words or text.
- Students will demonstrate automaticity of instructional-level words.

State Learning Goal

Say: *Today we will read an* **informational text**. *The purpose for reading the text is to read with* **accuracy** *and understanding. That means we will practice reading every word correctly and will understand what each word means. We will be aware when we do not understand the meaning of what we read, or are confused by a word or phrase.*

Ask: *What is the purpose for reading today? (I will read correctly, with accuracy, and know what each word means).*

Before Reading

Explain that readers have many strategies to be able to read and understand what they read. When they do not understand what they are reading, they stop and reread. They think about what they have read and determine meaning before continuing. If they cannot figure out the meaning of a word, they look for clues–such as the words around the word they do not know, and word parts that may provide a clue to the meaning of the word–to try to figure out the words.

Say: *We are going to practice reading each word correctly, making sure we understand the meaning of each word.*

Read the list of words and have students identify words they do not know. Using context clues, explain the meaning of unknown words. Redefine words as needed. Example:

Unknown Word	Word in Context	Word Redefined
(student-generated)	As it appears in sentence	- look at word parts (structural clues) - look up in dictionary (definition) - look at surrounding words (context clues) - determine if it is a cognate

During Reading

First Read: Teacher models rereading words correctly and fluently.

Second Read: Teacher uses the Recording Time Sheet BLM (61) to monitor the student's initial fluency and accuracy rate. Student reads each word on the list. Teacher identifies and annotates student's errors and self-corrections, and discusses word/phrase relationship to overall passage (multiple meanings, synonyms/antonyms, roots, affixes).

Third Read: Student reads the whole passage aloud to self or to partner with appropriate fluency and pacing. A second fluency and accuracy rate is recorded.

After Reading

Use the Comprehension Monitoring BLM (62) to monitor and record comprehension. Ask text-dependent questions to ensure student understanding. To check for comprehension, ask students to retell or explain the text in their own words. Ask questions such as:

- What is this text about?
- Recall two important facts or details you remember about _____.
  1) _____   2) _____
- Explain in your own words what the author is saying about _____.
- What idea does the author present first?
- What does the author tell us next?
- Why is this information important?
- Which piece of information is the most important? How do you know?
- What have you learned from reading this text?
- How does _____ relate to _____?
- How does this text conclude?

Conclusion

Ask: *What did we learn today?*

Say: *We learned how to read words correctly and understand what we read. When we read, it is important to read the words correctly and understand the meaning of the words we read.*

Use the Self-Evaluation BLM (63) for student self-reflection, evaluation, and goal setting.

Home Connection

Provide students with a copy of the text to take home to read to family members. Provide a copy of the Recording Time Sheet BLM (61) to take home, so that a family member can time and record the student's reading. Encourage students to ask their family members questions about the text.

✔ Formative Assessment

If the student completes each task correctly, proceed to the next skill in the sequence. If not, refer to suggested Intervention 2.

Did the student…?	Intervention 2
Recall the purpose for reading?	• Explain that a "purpose" is a "reason." Explain that we pay attention to how we read the text aloud so that it sounds like we are talking, so that we can understand what we are reading.
Listen attentively while the teacher modeled?	• Model reading fluently while students echo-or choral-read. Conduct a cloze read as student chimes in with missing words.
Read each sentence progressively?	• Guide students in reading the words, phrases, and sentences by scrolling the text to expose one line at a time while it is being read.
Scroll from one line to another effortlessly?	• Have students practice tracking each word and using the return sweep with their finger as you read aloud together.
Read informational text with appropriate pacing?	• Practice reading the word list and matching words from the list to the text.
Read informational text with appropriate intonation?	• Select a portion of the text that requires varied intonation to practice reading. Discuss the meaning, feelings, and thoughts conveyed by the text to explain why changing the tone of voice is necessary to express meaning and support understanding the text.

Read Literary Text with Understanding, Intonation, and Expression RF.3.4a

CCSS: RF.3.4
Read with sufficient accuracy and fluency to support comprehension.
a. Read on-level text with purpose and understanding.

Lesson Objectives

- Determine genre of text before reading and demonstrate understanding of the purpose for reading.
- Demonstrate an understanding of grade-appropriate vocabulary.
- Participate in guided/shared reading of different genres of text.
- Make and confirm predictions in text read aloud by the teacher.
- Read with intonation and expression.

Essential Question
How do readers know what kind of expression to use?

Metacognitive Strategy
Think while listening; plan, monitor and evaluate listening; reference pictures/visuals/illustrations to predict and confirm understanding.

Academic Language
Story, character, setting, events, details, retell, predict, sequence of events, first, next, then, last or finally

Additional Materials
- BLMs 16, 28, 40, 46, 52, Read for Understanding
- BLM 63, Self-Evaluation

Pre-Assess
Student's ability to listen with attention, understand what is being read aloud, and use picture clues

Student's understanding of how voice and expression are used to convey the meaning of a text being read aloud

Introduce

- Students will be aware of a specific purpose for listening and reading
- Students will demonstrate listening comprehension by responding to *wh-* questions or explaining what the text read aloud is about.
- Students will demonstrate listening retention by retelling—using illustrations and recalling words/phrases from the text.

State Learning Goal

Say: *Today we will read a* **story***. The purpose for listening will be to remember what the story is about, the sequence of* **events***, and the details we enjoyed. Listen to the sound and tone of my voice as it changes when I read aloud.*

Ask: *What is the purpose for listening today? (To remember what the story is about, to listen to voice changes)*

Before Read-Aloud

Use the title and illustrations to establish the main idea/theme and activate prior knowledge. Build background knowledge by discussing illustrations. Discuss text language and key vocabulary, if present, to make certain that students understand their meaning.

Ask: *What do you* **predict** *this story will be about? (Point out title and details in illustrations as clues to prediction.)*

During Read-Aloud

First Read: Model reading fluently at a natural pace, with intonation, rhythm, and expression. Include dramatic gestures and varied voice intonation during dialogue, if applicable, to engage students and facilitate comprehension. Model reading without intonation, rhythm, and expression.

Ask: Which reading did you like best? Why?

Second Read: Interactive reading while thinking aloud, asking thoughtful questions, emphasizing key details and confirm prediction.

- Ask and answer questions to demonstrate understanding of text. Cite text.
- Recount stories, determine main ideas, explain how information is conveyed through key details in text.

Describe **characters**–traits, motivation, and feelings–to explain how their actions contribute to the sequence of events. Third Read: Echo-read or choral-read with the student, emphasizing appropriate pacing, intonation, and expression.

Say: *When we read aloud, the sound of our voice also gives meaning to the words*

After Read-Aloud

Have students demonstrate understanding of text by asking them to retell the story in their own words using key details and referencing illustrations. Support students by providing question prompts relating to the sequence of events, such as: What happened first? Next? Then? Last?

Conclusion

Ask: *What did we learn today?*

Say: *We learned that when we read, our voice and expressions change along with the words. We read the same way we speak–not too quickly and not too slowly– so that we can understand what we read.*

Use the Self-Evaluation BLM (63) for student self-reflection, evaluation, and goal setting.

Home Connection

Ask students to take the story home to reread with a family member. Have students point out key details and events they remember and discuss with their family what the story is about.

✔Formative Assessment

If the student completes each task correctly, proceed to the next skill in the sequence. If not, refer to suggested Intervention 2.

Did the student…?	Intervention 2
Recall the purpose for listening?	• Explain that a "purpose" is a "reason." Explain that we pay attention to what is read with a reason. *Say: We will listen to remember what the story is about. We will remember key details and events.* (Provide examples.)
Connect to prior knowledge?	• Build new knowledge using illustrations, and provide personal examples that connect to what students already know.
Build understanding of vocabulary?	• Use visuals, quick sketches, gestures, and realia. Provide definitions and examples.
Predict what the story was about?	• Make connections between title, illustrations, and key vocabulary.
Recall key details and events?	• Use a story structure graphic organizer to sketch and analyze story elements.
Echo-or choral-read?	• Echo-read one phrase or sentence at a time, and check for understanding.
Retell story?	• Use sentence frames or sentence starters correlated to story events.

Read Literary Text with Accuracy, Appropriate Rate, and Expression RF.3.4b

CCSS: RF.3.4
Read with sufficient accuracy and fluency to support comprehension.
b. Read on-level prose and poetry orally with accuracy, appropriate rate, and expression on successive readings.

Prerequisite lesson: 2a

Lesson Objectives

- Listen to different genres being read aloud fluently.
- Read with accuracy, appropriate rate and expression.
- Decode instructional-level words with increasing automaticity.
- Read sight words accurately and automatically.
- Use phrasing/fluency technique.

Essential Questions
How does grouping words help you read better? How does punctuation help a reader?

Metacognitive Strategy
Use selective attention and monitor comprehension while reading.

Academic Language
Pacing, fluency, words, phrases

Additional Materials
- BLMs 17, 29, 41, 47, 53, Read for Expression
- BLM 63, Self Evaluation

Pre-Assess
Student's ability to decode instructional-level words with automaticity and to understand text while reading it aloud

Introduce

- Students will be aware of a specific purpose for reading.
- Students will read with proper phrasing and fluency.
- Students will demonstrate automaticity of instructional-level words.

State Learning Goal

Say: *Today we will read a* **story**. *The purpose for reading the story is to read with appropriate* **pacing** *and* **fluency**. *That means we will not read too quickly or too slowly, so that we can understand what we are reading. We will read* **words** *and* **phrases** *aloud so we can practice reading and understanding what we read.*

Ask: *What is the purpose for reading today? (I will read words and phrases aloud so I can understand what I read.)*

Before Reading

Explain that it is helpful to know when to pause while reading, and also how to read words that go together without stopping. Explain that students are going to read the story and practice pausing and reading words that go together naturally.

During Reading

First Read: Teacher models reading each sentence with proper phrasing and fluency. Teacher reads the whole passage, pointing out punctuation marks. Teacher rereads, asking students to listen to the changes in tone of voice.

Second Read: Student reads each sentence progressively, scrolling down each line of the story.

Third Read: Student reads the whole story with appropriate fluency and pacing. Teacher monitors for student's accuracy, fluency, and pacing.

After Reading

Have students read to partners to demonstrate that they can use the sentence progression strategy to practice appropriate fluency and pacing.

Conclusion

Ask: *What did we learn today?*

Say: *We learned how to pause while reading, and how to read phrases that go together naturally. We read as we speak—not too quickly and not too slowly—so that we can understand what we read. Punctuation helps readers know when to pause, stop, and change their tone of voice. Reading with appropriate pacing and intonation helps us understand what we read.*

Use the Self-Evaluation BLM (63) for student self-reflection, evaluation, and goal setting.

Home Connection
Ask students to take the story home to read with a family member. Have students practice the sentence progression strategy with members of their family.

✔ Formative Assessment

If the student completes each task correctly, proceed to the next skill in the sequence. If not, refer to suggested Intervention 2.

Did the student...?	Intervention 2
Recall the purpose for reading?	• Explain that a "purpose" is a "reason." Explain that we pay attention to how we read the text aloud so that is sounds like we are talking, so that we can understand what we are reading. *Say: We have to make sure that we are not reading too quickly or too slowly. We will read each word followed by the next until the words become a sentence that makes sense.*
Listen attentively while the teacher modeled?	• Model reading fluently while students echo-or choral-read. Conduct a cloze read as student chimes in with missing words.
Read each sentence progressively?	• Guide students in reading the words, phrases, and sentences by scrolling the text to expose one line at a time while it is being read.
Scroll from one line to another effortlessly?	• Have students practice tracking each word and using the return sweep with their finger as you read aloud together.
Read the story with appropriate pacing?	• Practice reading the word list and matching words from the list to the text.
Read the story with appropriate intonation?	• Select a portion of the text that requires varied intonation to practice reading. Discuss the meaning, feelings, and thoughts conveyed by the text to explain why changing the tone of voice is necessary to express meaning and support understanding the text.

Read Literary Text to Confirm Word Recognition and Understanding RF.3.4c

CCSS: RF.3.4
Read with sufficient accuracy and fluency to support comprehension.
c. Use context to confirm or self-correct word recognition and understanding, rereading as necessary.

Prerequisite lessons: 2a, 2b

Lesson Objectives

- Read with purpose and understanding, determining whether or not the text is understood.
- Read with accuracy and comprehension, determining if a word is misread.
- Use context to determine meaning.
- Decode instructional-level words with increasing automaticity.

Essential Questions

What do I do when I do not know what a word means? What is an appropriate rate when reading?

Metacognitive Strategy

Use selective attention and monitor comprehension while reading; make inferences and use context clues.

Academic Language

Accuracy, comprehension

Additional Materials

- BLMs 18, 30, 42, 48, 54, Recognize Words
- BLM 61, Recording Time Sheet
- BLM 62, Comprehension Monitoring
- BLM 63, Self-Evaluation

Pre-Assess

Student's ability to decode instructional-level words with automaticity and to understand text while reading it aloud

Introduce

- Students will be aware of a specific purpose for reading.
- Students will read with accuracy and understanding, determining when they do not understand the meaning of words or text.
- Students will demonstrate automaticity of instructional-level words.

State Learning Goal

Say: *Today we will read a* **story**. *The purpose for reading the story is to read with* **accuracy** *and understanding. That means we will practice reading every word correctly and will understand what each word means. We will be aware when we do not understand the meaning of what we read, or are confused by a word or phrase. When we do not understand what we read, we will stop to figure it out.*

Ask: *What is the purpose for reading today? (I will read correctly, with accuracy, and know what each word means.)*

Before Reading

Explain that readers have many strategies to understand what they read. When they do not understand what they are reading, they stop and reread. They think about what they have read and determine meaning before continuing. If they cannot figure out the meaning of a word, they look for clues—such as the words around the word they do not know, and word parts that may provide a clue to the meaning of the word—to try to figure out the words.

Say: *We are going to practice reading each word correctly, making sure we understand the meaning of each word.*

Teacher reads the list of words, and students identify words they do not know. Using context clues, the teacher explains the meaning of unknown words. Teacher redefines words as needed. Example:

Unknown Word	Word in Context	Word Redefined
(student-generated)	As it appears in sentence	<ul><li>look at word parts (structural clues)</li><li>look up in dictionary (definition)</li><li>look at surrounding words (context clues)</li><li>determine if it is a cognate</li></ul>

During Reading

First Read: Teacher models rereading words correctly and fluently.

Second Read: Teacher uses the Recording Time Sheet BLM (61) to monitor the student's initial fluency and accuracy rate. Student reads each word on list. Teacher identifies and annotates student's errors and self-corrections, and discusses word/phrase relationship to overall passage (multiple meanings, synonyms/antonyms, roots, affixes).

Third Read: Student reads the whole passage aloud to self or to partner with appropriate fluency and pacing. A second fluency and accuracy rate is recorded.

After Reading

Use the Comprehension Monitoring BLM (62) to monitor and record comprehension. Ask text-dependent questions to ensure student understanding. To check for comprehension, ask students to retell or explain the text in their own words. Ask questions such as:

- In your own words, what is this story about?
- What is the problem in the story? How do you know?
- Who are characters in this story? What are their names?
- Who is the main character? How do you know?
- What is the setting of this story? How do you know?
- What are the characters doing? How are they doing this? Why do you think they are doing this?
- What is the main idea of the story?
- Can this really happen? Why or why not?
- What happened first, next, then, last?

Conclusion

Ask: *What did we learn today?*

Say: *We learned that how to read words correctly and understand what we read. When we read, it is important to read the words correctly and understand the meaning of the words we read.*

Use the Self-Evaluation BLM (63) for student self-reflection, evaluation, and goal setting.

Home Connection

Provide students with a copy of the story to take home to read to family members. Provide a copy of the Recording Time Sheet BLM (61) to take home so that a family member can time and record the student's reading. Encourage students to ask their family members questions about the story.

✔ Formative Assessment

If the student completes each task correctly, proceed to the next skill in the sequence. If not, refer to suggested Intervention 2.

Did the student…?	Intervention 2
Recall the purpose for reading?	• Explain that a "purpose" is a "reason." Explain that we pay attention to how we read the text aloud so that it sounds like we are talking, so that we can understand what we are reading.
Listen attentively while the teacher modeled?	• Model reading fluently while students echo-or choral-read. Conduct a cloze read as student chimes in with missing words.
Read each sentence progressively?	• Guide students in reading the words, phrases, and sentences by scrolling the text to expose one line at a time while it is being read.
Scroll from one line to another effortlessly?	• Have students practice tracking each word and using the return sweep with their finger as you read aloud together.
Read story with appropriate pacing?	• Practice reading the word list and matching words from the list to the text.
Read story with appropriate intonation?	• Select a portion of the text that requires varied intonation to practice reading. Discuss the meaning, feelings and thoughts conveyed by the text to explain why changing the tone of voice is necessary to express meaning and support understanding the text.

Read Poetry with Understanding, Intonation, and Expression RF.3.4a

CCSS: RF.3.4
Read with sufficient accuracy and fluency to support comprehension.
a. Read on-level text with purpose and understanding.

Lesson Objectives

- Determine genre of text before reading.
- Determine purpose for reading.
- Demonstrate understanding of text that is read aloud by another (e.g., answer questions, retell story, explain what text was about).

Essential Question

How do we read a poem/song/ nursery rhyme with expression, purpose, and understanding?

Metacognitive Strategy

Think while listening; plan, monitor and evaluate listening; reference pictures/visuals/illustrations to predict and confirm understanding.

Academic Language

Poetry, poem, rhyming words, rhythm, pattern, intonation, expression

Additional Materials

- BLMs 1, 4, 13, 25, 37, 49, Read for Understanding
- BLM 63, Self-Evaluation

Pre-Assess

Student's ability to listen with attention, understand what is being read aloud, and use picture clues

Introduce

- Students will be aware of a specific purpose for listening (listen to rhyming words, rhythm, intonation of voice).
- Students will demonstrate understanding by responding to *wh-* questions or explaining what the poem is about.
- Students will demonstrate appropriate expression and intonation as they read the poem.

State Learning Goal

Say: *Today we will read a **poem**/song/nursery rhyme. The purpose for listening to the poem/song/nursery rhyme will be to remember what the poem/song/nursery rhyme is about, and to remember a word, phrase, or **rhyming words** we enjoyed. We will practice reading with **expression** and **intonation**. This means our voice will change as we read the words and bring them to life, so we can understand and enjoy what we read.*

Ask: *What is the purpose for listening today? (To remember what the poem/ song/nursery rhyme is about, to listen to voice changes)*

Before Read-Aloud

Use the title and illustrations to establish the theme or subject of the poem/song/ nursery rhyme and to activate prior knowledge. Build background knowledge by discussing illustrations. Discuss text language and key vocabulary to make certain student understand their meaning.

Ask: *What do you predict this poem/song/nursery rhyme will be about? (Point out details in illustrations and key vocabulary as clues to the prediction.)*

During Read-Aloud

First Read: Model reading fluently at a natural pace, with intonation, **rhythm**, and expression, including dramatic gestures. Emphasize rhythm and rhyming words. Next, read the poem/song/nursery rhyme in a monotone, pausing inappropriately.

Ask: *Which reading did you like best? Why?*

Explain: Poems express thoughts with interesting words. Poems are often written with words that rhyme and with phrases that have repeating rhythms. To learn the best way to read a poem/song/nursery rhyme, we read it several times.

Second Read: Interactive reading while thinking aloud, asking thoughtful questions, and emphasizing catchy phrases and words that rhyme. Ask questions such as:

- What is this poem/song/nursery rhyme about?
- What ideas do you think the poet/author wants to communicate?
- What words rhyme?
- Which words or phrases catch your attention?
- How does this poem/song/nursery rhyme make you feel?
- What thoughts come to your mind?

Third Read: Echo-read or choral-read with the student, emphasizing appropriate pacing, intonation, rhythm, and expression.

Say: *Lets practice reading the poem/song/nursery rhyme several times with rhythm and intonation. Let's use our voice to communicate what we think or what we feel when we express what the poet wrote.*

After Read-Aloud

Have students demonstrate understanding of the text by asking them to retell or explain the poem/song/nursery rhyme in their own words. Ask students to recall and tell why they enjoyed a word, a phrase, or a pair of rhyming words.

Conclusion

Ask: *What did we learn today?*

Say: *We learned that when we read poems/songs/nursery rhymes, our voice and expressions change along with the words. We pay special attention to rhyming words, and we follow the rhythm of the words as we read. We read to communicate the thoughts and feelings the poet wanted to convey.*

Use the Self-Evaluation BLM (63) for student self-reflection, evaluation, and goal setting.

✔ Formative Assessment

If the student completes each task correctly, proceed to the next skill in the sequence. If not, refer to suggested Intervention 2.

Did the student...?	Intervention 2
Recall the purpose for listening?	• Explain that a "purpose" is a "reason." Explain that we pay attention to what is read with a reason. *Say: We will listen to remember what the poem/song/nursery rhyme is about We will remember words we liked and rhyming words.* (Provide examples.)
Connect to prior knowledge?	• Build new knowledge using visuals, and provide personal examples that connect to what students already know.
Build understanding of vocabulary?	• Use visuals, quick sketches, gestures, and realia. Provide definitions and examples.
Predict what the poem/song/ nursery rhyme was about?	• Make connections between title, illustrations. and key vocabulary.
Recall rhyming words. phrases?	• Point out rhyming words, keywords, and phrases; have students echo-read them with you
Echo-or choral-read?	• Have students clap or sway to the rhythm of poem.

Read Poetry with Accuracy, Appropriate Rate, and Expression RF.3.4b

CCSS: RF.3.4
Read with sufficient accuracy and fluency to support comprehension.
b. Read on-level prose and poetry orally with accuracy, appropriate rate, and expression on successive readings.

Prerequisite lesson: 3a

Lesson Objectives

- Read with accuracy, appropriate rate, and expression.
- Distinguish between interrogative, declarative, and exclamatory sentences.
- Decode instructional-level words with increasing automaticity.
- Use phrasing techniques.

Metacognitive Strategy
Use selective attention and monitor comprehension while reading.

Academic Language
Pacing, fluency, words, phrases

Additional Materials
- BLMs 2, 5, 14, 26, 38, 50, Read for Expression
- BLM 63, Self-Evaluation

Pre-Assess
Student's ability to decode instructional-level words with automaticity and to understand text while reading it aloud

Introduce

- Students will be aware of a specific purpose for reading.

- Students will read with proper phrasing and fluency.

- Students will demonstrate automaticity of instructional-level words.

State Learning Goal

Say: *Today we will read a* **poem***/song/nursery rhyme. The purpose for reading the poem/song/nursery rhyme is to read with appropriate* **pacing** *and* **fluency***. That means we will not read too quickly or too slowly, so that we can understand what we are reading. We will read* **words** *and* **phrases** *aloud so we can practice reading and understanding what we read.*

Ask: *What is the purpose for reading today? (I will read words and phrases aloud so I can understand what I read.)*

Before Reading

Explain that it is helpful to know when to pause while reading, and also how to read words that go together without stopping. We are going to read the poem and practice pausing and reading words that go together naturally.

During Reading

First Read: Teacher models reading phrases, scrolling down each line as it is read.

Second Read: Student reads each phrase progressively, scrolling down each line as the sentences form.

Third Read: Student reads the whole poem/song/nursery rhyme with appropriate fluency and pacing.

After Reading

Have students read to partners to demonstrate that they are able to use the phrasing/fluency strategy to practice pausing and reading words that go together naturally.

Conclusion

Ask: *What did we learn today?*

Say: *We learned how to pause while reading, and how to read words that go together naturally. We read as we speak—not too quickly and not too slowly—so that we can understand what we read.*

Use the Self-Evaluation BLM (63) for student self-reflection, evaluation, and goal setting.

Home Connection

Ask students to take the poem/song/nursery rhyme home to read with a family member. Have students demonstrate the phrasing/fluency strategy to members of their family.

✔ Formative Assessment

If the student completes each task correctly, proceed to the next skill in the sequence. If not, refer to suggested Intervention 2.

Did the student...?	Intervention 2
Recall the purpose for reading?	• Explain that a "purpose" is a "reason." Explain that we pay attention to how we read the text aloud so that it sounds like we are talking, so that we can understand what we are reading.
Listen attentively while the teacher modeled?	• Model reading fluently while students echo-or choral-read. Conduct a cloze read as student chimes in with missing words.
Read each phrase progressively?	• Guide students in reading the words, phrases, and sentences by scrolling the text to expose one line at a time while it is being read.
Scroll from one line to another effortlessly?	• Have students practice tracking each word and using the return sweep with their finger as you read aloud together.
Read the poem/song/nursery rhyme with appropriate pacing?	• Guide students in clapping (swaying, marching, tapping on the table, etc.) to the rhythm of the poem/song/nursery rhyme as they read it together.
Read the poem/song/nursery rhyme with appropriate intonation?	• Orchestrate with hand gestures to mark the high and low tones of the poem/song/nursery rhyme. Students choral-read as teacher orchestrates.

Read Poetry to Confirm Word Recognition and Understanding RF.3.4c

CCSS: RF.3.4
Read with sufficient accuracy and fluency to support comprehension.
c. Use context to confirm or self-correct word recognition and understanding, rereading as necessary.

Prerequisite lessons: 3a, 3b

Lesson Objectives

- Read with purpose and understanding.
- Read with accuracy and comprehension.
- Decode instructional-level words with increasing automaticity.

Metacognitive Strategy
Use selective attention and monitor comprehension while reading.

Academic Language
Accuracy, comprehension

Additional Materials
- BLMs 3, 6, 15, 27, 39, 51, Recognize Words
- BLM 61, Recording Time Sheet
- BLM 62, Comprehension Monitoring
- BLM 63, Self-Evaluation

Pre-Assess
Student's ability to decode instructional-level words with automaticity and to understand text while reading it aloud

Introduce

- Students will be aware of a specific purpose for reading.

- Students will read with accuracy and understanding.

- Students will demonstrate automaticity of instructional-level words.

State Learning Goal

Say: *Today we will read a **poem**/song/nursery rhyme. The purpose for reading the poem/song/nursery rhyme is to read with **accuracy** and understanding. That means we will practice reading every word correctly and will understand what each word means.*

Ask: *What is the purpose for reading today? (I will read each word correctly and know what each word means.)*

Before Reading

Explain that readers have many strategies for reading and understanding what they read. When students do not understand what they are reading, they can stop and reread. They think about what they have read and determine meaning before continuing. If they cannot figure out the meaning of a word, students can look for clues—such as the words around the word they do not know, and word parts that may provide a clue to the meaning of the word they do not know.

Say: *We are going to practice reading each word correctly, making sure we understand the meaning of each word.*

Read the list of words and have students identify words they do not know. Using context clues, explain the meaning of unknown words. Redefine words as needed. Example:

Unknown Word	Word in Context	Word Redefined
(student-generated)	As it appears in sentence	• look at word parts (structural clues) • look up in dictionary (definition) • look at surrounding words (context clues) • determine if it is a cognate

During Reading

First Read: Teacher models reading words correctly and fluently.

Second Read: Teacher uses the Recording Time Sheet BLM (61) to monitor the student's initial fluency and accuracy rate. Student reads each word on the list. Teacher identifies and annotates student's errors and self-corrections, and discusses word/phrase relationship to overall passage (multiple meanings, synonyms/antonyms, roots, affixes).

Third Read: Student reads the whole passage aloud to self or to partner with appropriate fluency and pacing. A second fluency and accuracy rate is recorded.

After Reading

Use the Comprehension Monitoring BLM (62) to monitor and record comprehension. Ask text-dependent questions to ensure student understanding. To check for comprehension, ask students to retell or explain text in their own words. Ask questions such as:

- In your own words, what is this poem/song/nursery rhyme about?
- Who are characters in this poem/song/nursery rhyme? What are their names?
- What is the setting of this poem/song/nursery rhyme? How do you know?
- What is a detail in the poem/song/nursery rhyme that tells you what the poem/song/nursery rhyme is a about?
- What are they doing? How are they doing this? Why do you think they are doing this?
- What is the most interesting line in the poem/song/nursery rhyme? Why?
- What does the writer mean by _____? How do you know?
- Can this really happen? Why or why not?
- What are some rhyming words in the poem/song/nursery rhyme?

Conclusion

Ask: *What did we learn today?*

Say: *We learned how to read words correctly and understand what we read. When we read, it is important to read the words correctly and understand the meaning of the words we read.*

Use the Self-Evaluation BLM (63) for student self-reflection, evaluation, and goal setting.

Home Connection

Provide students with a copy of the poem/song/nursery rhyme to take home to read to family members. Provide a copy of Recording Time Sheet BLM (61) to take home so that a family member can time and record the student's reading. Encourage students to ask their family members questions about the poem.

✔ Formative Assessment

If the student completes each task correctly, proceed to the next skill in the sequence. If not, refer to suggested Intervention 2.

Did the student…?	Intervention 2
Recall the purpose for reading?	• Explain that a "purpose" is a "reason." Explain that we pay attention to how we read the text aloud so that it sounds like we are talking so that we can understand what we are reading. *Say: We have to make sure that we are not reading too quickly or too slowly. We will read each word followed by the next until the words become a sentence that makes sense.*
Listen attentively while the teacher modeled?	• Model reading fluently while students echo-or choral-read. Conduct a cloze read as student chimes in with missing words.
Read each phrase progressively?	• Guide students in reading the words, phrases, and sentences by scrolling the text to expose one line at a time while it is being read.
Scroll from one line to another effortlessly?	• Have students practice tracking each word and using the return sweep with their finger as you read aloud together.
Read the poem with appropriate pacing?	• Guide students in clapping (swaying, marching, tapping on the table, etc.) to the rhythm of poem as they read the poem together.
Read the poem with appropriate intonation?	• Orchestrate with hand gestures to mark the high and low tones of the poem. Students choral-read as teacher orchestrates.

Read Drama with Understanding, Intonation, and Expression RF.3.4a

CCSS: RF.3.4
Read with sufficient accuracy and fluency to support comprehension.
a. Read on-level text with purpose and understanding.

Lesson Objectives

- Determine genre of text before reading.
- Determine purpose for reading.
- Use expression to reflect understanding and interpretation of the text.

Essential Question

How do we read a play with expression, purpose, and understanding?

Metacognitive Strategy

Think while listening/reading; plan, monitor, and interpret text; make personal connections with the text.

Academic Language

Theatre, play, acting, voice, pattern, intonation, expression, lines, dialogue, script

Additional Materials

- Pre-selected drama text (Teacher should select a drama text based on students' ages and reading levels, and on the number of students in the class).
- BLM 63, Self-Evaluation

Pre-Assess

Student's ability to listen with attention, understand what is being read aloud, and follow a script

Introduce

- Students will be aware of a specific purpose for listening (listen and follow dialogue, intonation of voice).

- Students will demonstrate understanding by responding to *wh-* questions or explaining what the play is about.

- Students will demonstrate appropriate expression and intonation as they interpret characters.

State Learning Goal

Say: *Today we will read part of a* **play**. *The purpose for listening and reading will be to interpret—or pretend to be—the characters in the play. You will use your* **voice**, **expressions**, *and gestures to show that you understand your assigned character. You will also pay attention and follow along as other readers read their character's* **lines**.

Ask: *What is the purpose for listening and reading today? (to read as we pretend we are characters in a play)*

Before Read-Aloud

Use the title and illustrations, if present, to establish the theme or subject of the play and to activate prior knowledge. Build background knowledge by discussing illustrations, text language, and key vocabulary to make certain that students understand their meaning. Review the characters and have students predict by describing what each character voice, actions, and personality may be like. Explain that the narrator is the person who tells or narrates parts of the story to the audience.

Ask: *What do you predict this play will be about? (Point out details in illustration, key vocabulary as clues to prediction.)*

During Read-Aloud

First Read: Model reading fluently at a natural pace, with **intonation**, rhythm, and expression, including dramatic gestures. Point to each character's lines in the **script** and vary the voice of each character.

Ask: *Which character did you like best? Why?*

Second Read: Interactive reading while thinking aloud, asking thoughtful questions, and emphasizing catchy phrases and body movements to convey and interpret meaning. Ask questions such as:

- What is this play about?
- What are the characters thinking and feeling?
- How do you know?
- Have you ever felt, thought or acted like any of these characters?

Third Read: Echo-read or choral-read, emphasizing expression and a different voice intonation for each character.

Say: *Let's practice reading the play, giving each character a different voice. We will use our voices to interpret and reflect what we think or what we feel when we express what the author wrote.*

After Read-Aloud

Have students demonstrate understanding of the text by retelling or explaining the play in their own words. Motivate students to collaborate with others to practice and perform the script for the class.

Conclusion

Ask: *What did we learn today?*

Say: *We learned that when we read scripts, we use our voice and expressions to pretend we are the characters in the play. We learned that a script is text that is written in **dialogue** showing what each character says. In parts of the play, the narrator reads the lines that narrate—or tell—the story to the audience.*

Use the Self-Evaluation BLM (63) for student self-reflection, evaluation, and goal setting.

Home Connection

Ask students to take the script home to read with a family member. Encourage students to invite members of the family to read and perform the play with them.

✔ Formative Assessment

If the student completes each task correctly, proceed to the next skill in the sequence. If not, refer to suggested Intervention 2.

Did the student…?	Intervention 2
Recall the purpose for listening?	• Explain that a "purpose" is a "reason." Explain that we pay attention to what is read for a reason. Say: *We will listen to remember what the play is about, we listen to follow the script.*
Connect to prior knowledge?	• Build new knowledge using visuals, and provide personal examples that connect to what students already know.
Build understanding of vocabulary?	• Use visuals, gestures, and realia. Provide definitions and examples.
Predict what play was about?	• Make connections between title, key vocabulary, and illustrations
Read with expression?	• Have students think about the characters and put themselves in those situations. Discuss characters' thoughts and feelings. Model acting out the words to reflect characters' thoughts, feelings and actions.
Echo-or choral-read?	• Have student follow along, tracking with index finger as the words are read. Have student echo short lines, or parts of lines. Have student chime in with keywords, phrases or expressions.

Read Drama with Accuracy, Appropriate Rate, and Expression RF.3.4

CCSS: RF.3.4
Read with sufficient accuracy and fluency to support comprehension.
b. Read on-level prose and poetry orally with accuracy, appropriate rate, and expression on successive readings.

Prerequisite lesson: 4a

Lesson Objectives

- Read with accuracy, appropriate rate, and expression.
- Distinguish between interrogative, declarative, and exclamatory sentences.
- Decode instructional-level words with increasing automaticity.
- Use phrasing techniques.

Metacognitive Strategy
Use selective attention and monitor comprehension while reading.

Academic Language
Pacing, fluency, words, phrases

Additional Materials

- Pre-selected drama text (Teacher should select a drama text based on students' ages and reading levels, and on the number of students in the class).
- BLM 63, Self-Evaluation

Pre-Assess

Student's ability to decode instructional-level words with automaticity and to understand text while reading it aloud

Introduce

- Students will be aware of a specific purpose for reading.
- Students will read with proper phrasing and fluency.
- Students will demonstrate automaticity of instructional-level words.

State Learning Goal

Say: *Today we will read part of a **play**. The purpose for reading is to read with appropriate **pacing** and **fluency**. That means we will not read too quickly or too slowly, so that we can understand what we are reading. We will read **words** and **phrases** aloud so we can practice reading and understanding what we read.*

Ask: *What is the purpose for reading today? (I will read words and phrases aloud so I can understand what I read.)*

Before Reading

Explain that it is helpful to know when to pause while reading, and also how to read words that go together without stopping. Explain that students are going to read the play and practice pausing and reading words that go together naturally.

During Reading

First Read: Teacher models reading phrases, scrolling down each line as it is read.

Second Read: Student reads each phrase progressively, scrolling down each line as the sentences form.

Third Read: Student reads the whole play with appropriate fluency and pacing.

After Reading

Have students read to partners to demonstrate that they are able to use the phrasing/fluency strategy to practice pausing and reading words that go together naturally.

Conclusion

Ask: *What did we learn today?*

Say: *We learned how to pause while reading, and how to read words that go together naturally. We read as we speak—not too quickly and not too slowly—so that we can understand what we read.*

Use the Self-Evaluation BLM (63) for student self-reflection, evaluation, and goal setting.

Home Connection

Ask students to take the play home to read with a family member. Have students demonstrate the phrasing/fluency strategy to members of their family.

✔ Formative Assessment

If the student completes each task correctly, proceed to the next skill in the sequence. If not, refer to suggested Intervention 2.

Did the student...?	Intervention 2
Recall the purpose for reading?	• Explain that a "purpose" is a "reason." Explain that we pay attention to how we read the text aloud so that it sounds like we are talking, so that we can understand what we are reading.
Listen attentively while the teacher modeled?	• Model reading fluently while students echo-or choral-read. Conduct a cloze read as student chimes in with missing words.
Read each phrase progressively?	• Guide students in reading the words, phrases, and sentences by scrolling the text to expose one line at a time while it is being read.
Scroll from one line to another effortlessly?	• Have students practice tracking each word and using the return sweep with their finger as you read aloud together.
Read the play with appropriate pacing?	• Guide students in clapping (swaying, marching, tapping on the table, etc.) to the rhythm of the play as they read it together.
Read the play with appropriate intonation?	• Orchestrate with hand gestures to mark the high and low tones of the piece. Students choral-read as teacher orchestrates.

CCSS: RF.3.4
Read with sufficient accuracy and fluency to support comprehension.
c. Use context to confirm or self-correct word recognition and understanding, rereading as necessary.

Prerequisite lessons: 4a, 4b

Lesson Objectives

- Read with purpose and understanding.
- Read with accuracy and comprehension.
- Decode instructional-level words with increasing automaticity.

Metacognitive Strategy
- Use selective attention and monitor comprehension while reading.

Academic Language
Accuracy, comprehension

Additional Materials
- Pre-selected drama text (Teacher should select a drama text based on students' ages and reading levels, and on the number of students in the class).
- BLM 61, Recording Time Sheet
- BLM 62, Comprehension Monitoring
- BLM 63, Self-Evaluation

Pre-Assess
Student's ability to decode instructional-level words with automaticity and to understand text while reading it aloud

Read Drama to Confirm Word Recognition and Understanding RF.3.4

Introduce
- Students will be aware of a specific purpose for reading.
- Students will read with accuracy and understanding.
- Students will demonstrate automaticity of instructional-level words.

State Learning Goal

Say: *Today we will read part of a* **play**. *The purpose for reading the play is to read with* **accuracy** *and understanding. That means we will practice reading every word correctly and will understand what each word means.*

Ask: *What is the purpose for reading today? (I will read each word correctly and know what each word means.)*

Before Reading

Explain that readers have many strategies for reading and understanding what they read. When students do not understand what they are reading, they can stop and reread. They think about what they have read and determine meaning before continuing. If they cannot figure out the meaning of a word, students can look for clues—such as the words around the word they do not know and word parts that may provide a clue to the meaning of the word they do not know—to try to figure out the words.

Say: *We are going to practice reading each word correctly, making sure we understand the meaning of each word.*

Read the list of words and have students identify words they do not know. Using context clues, explain the meaning of unknown words. Redefine words as needed. Example:

Unknown Word	Word in Context	Word Redefined
(student-generated)	As it appears in sentence	• look at word parts (structural clues) • look up in dictionary (definition) • look at surrounding words (context clues) • determine if it is a cognate

During Reading

First Read: Teacher models reading words correctly and fluently.

Second Read: Teacher uses the Recording Time Sheet BLM (61) to monitor the student's initial fluency and accuracy rate. Student reads each word on the list. Teacher identifies and annotates student's errors and self-corrections, and discusses word/phrase relationship to overall passage (multiple meanings, synonyms/antonyms, roots, affixes).

Third Read: Student reads the whole passage aloud to self or to partner with appropriate fluency and pacing. A second fluency and accuracy rate is recorded.

After Reading

Use the Comprehension Monitoring BLM (62) to monitor and record comprehension. Ask text-dependent questions to ensure student understanding. To check for comprehension, ask students to retell or explain the text in their own words. Ask questions such as:

- In your own words, what is this play about?
- How does the play begin? Where does the play begin?
- Who are characters in this play? What are their names?
- What did _____ mean when he/she said _____?
- What do you learn about the characters from their first few lines?
- What are the stage directions? Why are they important?
- What is the setting of this play? How do you know?
- What are they doing? How are they doing this? Why do you think they are doing this?
- Can this really happen? Why or why not?
- How does the play end? Where does the play end?

Conclusion

Ask: *What did we learn today?*

Say: *We learned how to read words correctly and understand what we read. When we read, it is important to read the words correctly and understand the meaning of the words we read.*

Use the Self-Evaluation BLM (63) for student self-reflection, evaluation, and goal setting.

Home Connection

Provide students with a copy of the play to take home to read to family members. Provide a copy of the Recording Time Sheet BLM (61) to take home so that a family member can time and record the student's reading. Encourage students to ask their family members questions about the play.

✔ Formative Assessment

If the student completes each task correctly, proceed to the next skill in the sequence. If not, refer to suggested Intervention 2.

Did the student…?	Intervention 2
Recall the purpose for reading?	• Explain that a "purpose" is a "reason." Explain that we pay attention to how we read the text aloud so that it sounds like we are talking, so that we can understand what we are reading.
Listen attentively while the teacher modeled?	• Model reading fluently while students echo- or choral-read. Conduct a cloze read as student chimes in with missing words.
Read each phrase progressively?	• Guide students in reading the words, phrases, and sentences by scrolling the text to expose one line at a time while it is being read.
Scroll from one line to another effortlessly?	• Have students practice tracking each word and using the return sweep with their finger as you read aloud together.
Read the play with appropriate pacing?	• Guide students in clapping (swaying, marching, tapping on the table, etc.) to the rhythm of the play as they read it together.
Read the play with appropriate intonation?	• Orchestrate with hand gestures to mark the high and low tones of the play. Students choral-read as teacher orchestrates.

Name _____ **Date** _____

I Had a Little Nut Tree

I had a little nut tree,

Nothing would it bear

But a silver nutmeg

And a golden pear;

The King of Spain's daughter

Came to visit me,

And all for the sake

Of my little nut tree.

Her dress was made of crimson,

Jet black was her hair,

She asked me for my nutmeg

And my golden pear.

I said, "So fair a princess

Never did I see,

I'll give you all the fruit

From my little nut tree."

Name _____   Date _____

I

I had

I had a

I had a little

I had a little nut

I had a little nut tree,

Nothing

Nothing would

Nothing would it

Nothing would it bear

But

But a

But a silver

But a silver nutmeg

And

And a

And a golden

And a golden pear;

I Had a Little Nut Tree

I had a little nut tree,

Nothing would it bear

But a silver nutmeg

And a golden pear;

The King of Spain's daughter

Came to visit me,

And all for the sake

Of my little nut tree.

Her dress was made of crimson,

Jet black was her hair,

She asked me for my nutmeg

And my golden pear.

I said, "So fair a princess

Never did I see,

I'll give you all the fruit

From my little nut tree."

Name _____   Date _____

I	**I Had a Little Nut Tree**
it	I had a little nut tree,
and	Nothing would it bear
but	But a silver nutmeg
had	And a golden pear;
bear	
pear	The King of Spain's daughter
tree	Came to visit me,
would	And all for the sake
golden	Of my little nut tree.
nutmeg	
silver	Her dress was made of crimson,
nothing	Jet black was her hair,
	She asked me for my nutmeg
	And my golden pear.
	I said, "So fair a princess
	Never did I see,
	I'll give you all the fruit
	From my little nut tree."

Name _____ **Date** _____

excerpt from "Try, Try Again"
by T. H. Palmer

If we strive, 'tis no disgrace

Though we do not win the race;

What should you do in the case?

Try, try again.

If you find your task is hard,

Time will bring you your reward,

Try, try again.

All that other folks can do,

Why, with patience, should not you?

Only keep this rule in view:

Try, try again.

Name _____   **Date** _____

If

If we

If we strive,

If we strive, 'tis

If we strive, 'tis no

If we strive, 'tis no disgrace

Though

Though we

Though we do

Though we do not

Though we do not win

Though we do not win the

Though we do not win the race;

excerpt from "Try, Try Again"
by T. H. Palmer

If we strive, 'tis no disgrace

Though we do not win the race;

What should you do in the case?

Try, try again.

If you find your task is hard,

Time will bring you your reward,

Try, try again.

All that other folks can do,

Why, with patience, should not you?

Only keep this rule in view:

Try, try again.

Name _____ Date _____

do

if

in

no

we

not

'tis

try

you

case

race

what

wind

again

should

strive

though

disgrace

excerpt from "Try, Try Again"
by T. H. Palmer

If we strive, 'tis no disgrace

Though we do not win the race;

What should you do in the case?

Try, try again.

If you find your task is hard,

Time will bring you your reward,

Try, try again.

All that other folks can do,

Why, with patience, should not you?

Only keep this rule in view:

Try, try again.

Name _____ **Date** _____

Louis Pasteur

Louis Pasteur was a scientist.
He lived long ago. Pasteur
studied bacteria. Bacteria
are tiny things. He learned
that some bacteria cause
disease. These disease-causing
bacteria are called germs.
He learned that germs can
get inside people's bodies.
They can do this when people
have a cut. They can do this
when people eat food that
has germs on it. He proved
that people get sick from
germs. Many people did not
believe it. They did not think
tiny germs could kill larger
living things such as humans.
Pasteur found ways to kill
germs. He helped improve
people's health.

Name _____ Date _____

Louis

Louis Pasteur

Louis Pasteur was

Louis Pasteur was a

Louis Pasteur was a scientist.

He

He lived

He lived long

He lived long ago.

Pasteur

Pasteur studied

Pasteur studied bacteria.

Bacteria

Bacteria are

Bacteria are tiny

Bacteria are tiny things.

Louis Pasteur

Louis Pasteur was a scientist. He lived long ago. Pasteur studied bacteria. Bacteria are tiny things. He learned that some bacteria cause disease. These disease-causing bacteria are called germs. He learned that germs can get inside people's bodies. They can do this when people have a cut. They can do this when people eat food that has germs on it. He proved that people get sick from germs. Many people did not believe it. They did not think tiny germs could kill larger living things such as humans. Pasteur found ways to kill germs. He helped improve people's health.

Name _____   **Date** _____

ago

long

some

that

tiny

cause

lived

things

disease

studied

bacteria

scientist

Louis Pasteur

Louis Pasteur

Louis Pasteur was a scientist. He lived long ago. Pasteur studied bacteria. Bacteria are tiny things. He learned that some bacteria cause disease. These disease-causing bacteria are called germs. He learned that germs can get inside people's bodies. They can do this when people have a cut. They can do this when people eat food that has germs on it. He proved that people get sick from germs. Many people did not believe it. They did not think tiny germs could kill larger living things such as humans. Pasteur found ways to kill germs. He helped improve people's health.

Name _____ **Date** _____

adapted from "The Flies and the Pot of Honey" *by*
Horace E. Scudder

A Pot of Honey was overturned in the pantry. The Flies clustered about to eat the honey. But owing to the stickiness of the sweet stuff, they could not get away. Their feet were so stuck that they could not fly up.

So it is that greediness is for many people the cause of their ill-fortune.

Name _____   Date _____

A

A Pot

A Pot of

A Pot of Honey

A Pot of Honey was

A Pot of Honey was overturned

A Pot of Honey was overturned in

A Pot of Honey was overturned in the

A Pot of Honey was overturned in the pantry.

The

The Flies

The Flies clustered

The Flies clustered about

The Flies clustered about to

The Flies clustered about to eat

The Flies clustered about to eat the

The Flies clustered about to eat the honey.

adapted from "The Flies and the Pot of Honey"

by Horace E. Scudder

A Pot of Honey was overturned in the pantry. The Flies clustered about to eat the honey. But owing to the stickiness of the sweet stuff, they could not get away. Their feet were so stuck that they could not fly up.

So it is that greediness is for many people the cause of their ill-fortune.

Name _____   **Date** _____

in

of

up

eat

pot

the

was

about

flies

honey

pantry

clustered

overturned

adapted from "The Flies and the Pot of Honey"

by Horace E. Scudder

A Pot of Honey was overturned in the pantry. The Flies clustered about to eat the honey. But owing to the stickiness of the sweet stuff, they could not get away. Their feet were so stuck that they could not fly up.

So it is that greediness is for many people the cause of their ill-fortune.

Name _____   Date _____

The Wheels on the Bus

The wheels on the bus go

round and round,

round and round,

round and round.

The wheels on the bus go

round and round

all through the town.

The horn on the bus goes

beep, beep, beep,

beep, beep, beep,

beep, beep, beep.

The horn on the bus goes

beep, beep, beep

all through the town.

Name _____ **Date** _____

The

The wheels

The wheels on

The wheels on the

The wheels on the bus

The wheels on the bus go

round

round and

round and round,

round

round and

round and round,

round

round and

round and round.

The Wheels on the Bus

The wheels on the bus go

round and round,

round and round,

round and round.

The wheels on the bus go

round and round

all through the town.

The horn on the bus goes

beep, beep, beep,

beep, beep, beep,

beep, beep, beep.

The horn on the bus goes

beep, beep, beep

all through the town.

Name _____   Date _____

go

on

all

and

bus

the

beep

goes

horn

town

round

wheels

through

The Wheels on the Bus

The wheels on the bus go

round and round,

round and round,

round and round.

The wheels on the bus go

round and round

all through the town.

The horn on the bus goes

beep, beep, beep,

beep, beep, beep,

beep, beep, beep.

The horn on the bus goes

beep, beep, beep

all through the town.

Name _____ **Date** _____

Lost Dog

One day Erica came home from the park. Her dog, Zak, was not there. He had made a hole under the fence and run away. Erica and her dad went looking for Zak. They walked all around. They looked high and low.

"We are lost, too!" said Erica's dad.

"It's OK, Dad," said Erica. "Zak will take us home. Just look, he is sniffing his way back home right now!"

Name _____   Date _____

One

One day

One day Erica

One day Erica came

One day Erica came home

One day Erica came home
from

One day Erica came home
from the

One day Erica came home
from the park.

Her

Her dog,

Her dog, Zak,

Her dog, Zak, was

Her dog, Zak, was not

Her dog, Zak, was not there.

Lost Dog

One day Erica came home
from the park. Her dog, Zak,
was not there. He had made a
hole under the fence and run
away. Erica and her dad went
looking for Zak. They walked
all around. They looked high
and low.

"We are lost, too!" said Erica's
dad.

"It's OK, Dad," said Erica. "Zak
will take us home. Just look,
he is sniffing his way back
home right now!"

Name _____ **Date** _____

day

dog

her

one

run

the

Zak

high

hole

home

Erika

fence

around

walked

Lost Dog

One day Erica came home from the park. Her dog, Zak, was not there. He had made a hole under the fence and run away. Erica and her dad went looking for Zak. They walked all around. They looked high and low.

"We are lost, too!" said Erica's dad.

"It's OK, Dad," said Erica. "Zak will take us home. Just look, he is sniffing his way back home right now!"

Name _____ **Date** _____

excerpt from "The Ant-Hill"

from Wild Life in Woods and Fields
by Arabella B. Buckley

There is a big ant hill in the woods on the way to school. It is at the foot of the old oak tree, near the path, and is almost as tall as Peter. It looks like a loose heap of leaves, mixed with sticks and earth. It is broad at the bottom, and round at the top.

When we come home in the evening all is quiet on the ant-hill. We cannot see even one ant outside. It looks as if no one lived there. But when we pass in the morning, and the sun is warm and bright, we can see the ants creeping out of the cracks and running about the heap.

They are as big as grains of barley, and have a tiny knob in the middle of their body.

Name _____   Date _____

There

There is

There is a

There is a big

There is a big ant

There is a big ant hill

There is a big ant hill in

There is a big ant hill in the

There is a big ant hill in the woods

There is a big ant hill in the woods on

There is a big ant hill in the woods on the

There is a big ant hill in the woods on the way

There is a big ant hill in the woods on the way to

There is a big ant hill in the woods on the way to school.

excerpt from "The Ant-Hill"
from Wild Life in Woods and Fields by Arabella B. Buckley

There is a big ant hill in the woods on the way to school. It is at the foot of the old oak tree, near the path, and is almost as tall as Peter. It looks like a loose heap of leaves, mixed with sticks and earth. It is broad at the bottom, and round at the top.

When we come home in the evening all is quiet on the ant-hill. We cannot see even one ant outside. It looks as if no one lived there. But when we pass in the morning, and the sun is warm and bright, we can see the ants creeping out of the cracks and running about the heap.

They are as big as grains of barley, and have a tiny knob in the middle of their body.

Name _____ **Date** _____

as

in

of

big

oak

old

way

near

path

tall

tree

Peter

woods

almost

ant hill

school

excerpt from "The Ant-Hill"
from Wild Life in Woods and Fields by Arabella B. Buckley

There is a big ant hill in the woods on the way to school. It is at the foot of the old oak tree, near the path, and is almost as tall as Peter. It looks like a loose heap of leaves, mixed with sticks and earth. It is broad at the bottom, and round at the top.

When we come home in the evening all is quiet on the ant-hill. We cannot see even one ant outside. It looks as if no one lived there. But when we pass in the morning, and the sun is warm and bright, we can see the ants creeping out of the cracks and running about the heap.

They are as big as grains of barley, and have a tiny knob in the middle of their body.

Name _____   Date _____

Plant and Animal Partners

Many plants and animals depend on each other in order to survive.

For example, some birds eat fruit. The fruit grows on plants. The bird eats the fruit. The fruit contains seeds. But the bird cannot digest the seeds. The bird has seeds in its waste. The bird flies to different places. When it gets rid of its waste, it is helping spread the plant's seeds.

Squirrels also help plants. They bury nuts. If they forget where they buried a nut, the nut might grow into a new tree. The tree gives the squirrel food to eat. The squirrel helps plant the tree's seeds.

Name _____ Date _____

Many

Many plants

Many plants and

Many plants and animals

Many plants and animals depend

Many plants and animals depend on

Many plants and animals depend on each

Many plants and animals depend on each other

Many plants and animals depend on each other in

Many plants and animals depend on each other in order

Many plants and animals depend on each other in order to

Many plants and animals depend on each other in order to survive.

Plant and Animal Partners

Many plants and animals depend on each other in order to survive.

For example, some birds eat fruit. The fruit grows on plants. The bird eats the fruit. The fruit contains seeds. But the bird cannot digest the seeds. The bird has seeds in its waste. The bird flies to different places. When it gets rid of its waste, it is helping spread the plant's seeds.

Squirrels also help plants. They bury nuts. If they forget where they buried a nut, the nut might grow into a new tree. The tree gives the squirrel food to eat. The squirrel helps plant the tree's seeds.

Name _____ **Date** _____

eat

for

each

many

some

birds

fruit

order

depend

plants

animals

example

survive

Plant and Animal Partners

Many plants and animals depend on each other in order to survive.

For example, some birds eat fruit. The fruit grows on plants. The bird eats the fruit. The fruit contains seeds. But the bird cannot digest the seeds. The bird has seeds in its waste. The bird flies to different places. When it gets rid of its waste, it is helping spread the plant's seeds.

Squirrels also help plants. They bury nuts. If they forget where they buried a nut, the nut might grow into a new tree. The tree gives the squirrel food to eat. The squirrel helps plant the tree's seeds.

Name _____   Date _____

Little White Lily
by George Macdonald

Little White Lily

Sat by a stone,

Drooping and waiting

Till the sun shone.

Little White Lily

Sunshine has fed;

Little White Lily

Is lifting her head.

Little White Lily

Said: "It is good

Little White Lily's

Clothing and food."

Little White Lily

Dressed like a bride!

Shining with whiteness

And crowned beside!

Name _____   Date _____

Little

Little White

Little White Lily

Sat

Sat by

Sat by a

Sat by a stone,

Drooping

Drooping and

Drooping and waiting

Till

Till the

Till the sun

Till the sun shone.

Little White Lily
by George Macdonald

Little White Lily

Sat by a stone,

Drooping and waiting

Till the sun shone.

Little White Lily

Sunshine has fed;

Little White Lily

Is lifting her head.

Little White Lily

Said: "It is good

Little White Lily's

Clothing and food."

Little White Lily

Dressed like a bride!

Shining with whiteness

And crowned beside!

Name _____ **Date** _____

by

fed

has

sat

sun

the

'til

head

lily

shone

stone

white

lifting

waiting

drooping

sunshine

Little White Lily
by George Macdonald

Little White Lily

Sat by a stone,

Drooping and waiting

Till the sun shone.

Little White Lily

Sunshine has fed;

Little White Lily

Is lifting her head.

Little White Lily

Said: "It is good

Little White Lily's

Clothing and food."

Little White Lily

Dressed like a bride!

Shining with whiteness

And crowned beside!

Name _____ Date _____

The Tree House

Larry and his grandpa built a tree
house that looked like a rocket.
Larry wanted his friend to visit
the tree house. But Antonio was
in a wheelchair, so Grandpa built
something special for the tree
house.

Antonio came over to see the
tree house. Larry helped him get
on the special ramp. Then Larry
cried, "Blast off!"

Larry and Grandpa pulled the
rope, and Antonio went into the
tree house. Antonio liked riding
on the special ramp. But he liked
being in the tree house more!

Name _____ Date _____

Larry

Larry and

Larry and his

Larry and his grandpa

Larry and his grandpa built

Larry and his grandpa built a

Larry and his grandpa built a tree

Larry and his grandpa built a tree house

Larry and his grandpa built a tree house that

Larry and his grandpa built a tree house that looked

Larry and his grandpa built a tree house that looked like

Larry and his grandpa built a tree house that looked like a

Larry and his grandpa built a tree house that looked like a rocket.

The Tree House

Larry and his grandpa built a tree house that looked like a rocket. Larry wanted his friend to visit the tree house. But Antonio was in a wheelchair, so Grandpa built something special for the tree house.

Antonio came over to see the tree house. Larry helped him get on the special ramp. Then Larry cried, "Blast off!"

Larry and Grandpa pulled the rope, and Antonio went into the tree house. Antonio liked riding on the special ramp. But he liked being in the tree house more!

Name _____ **Date** _____

his

like

that

tree

built

house

Larry

visit

friend

looked

rocket

wanted

grandpa

The Tree House

Larry and his grandpa built a tree house that looked like a rocket. Larry wanted his friend to visit the tree house. But Antonio was in a wheelchair, so Grandpa built something special for the tree house.

Antonio came over to see the tree house. Larry helped him get on the special ramp. Then Larry cried, "Blast off!"

Larry and Grandpa pulled the rope, and Antonio went into the tree house. Antonio liked riding on the special ramp. But he liked being in the tree house more!

Name _____ Date _____

excerpt from "Spring Flowers"
by Arabella B. Buckley

We are always glad when April comes. Then we can find many flowers on our way to school. Even in February there are snowdrops in the orchard and Peter knows where he can sometimes find a primrose or violet in flower.

But we cannot get a good bunch until April. Before that the plants are busy growing their leaves.

The first bright flowers we find are daffodils in the fields, and the anemones in the woods. . . . They have very long, narrow leaves which come straight out of the ground. Each flower hangs on its own tall stalk. It has deep yellow tube in the middle, with a crown of pale yellow leaves round it.

Name _____   Date _____

We

We are

We are always

We are always glad

We are always glad when

We are always glad when
April

We are always glad when
April comes.

excerpt from "Spring Flowers"
by Arabella B. Buckley

We are always glad when April comes. Then we can find many flowers on our way to school. Even in February there are snowdrops in the orchard and Peter knows where he can sometimes find a primrose or violet in flower.

But we cannot get a good bunch until April. Before that the plants are busy growing their leaves.

The first bright flowers we find are daffodils in the fields, and the anemones in the woods. . . . They have very long, narrow leaves which come straight out of the ground. Each flower hangs on its own tall stalk. It has deep yellow tube in the middle, with a crown of pale yellow leaves round it.

Name _____   **Date** _____

I

we

are

can

way

find

glad

good

many

April

bunch

knows

Peter

plant

flower

leaves

school

violet

orchard

primrose

snowdrops

excerpt from "Spring Flowers"
by Arabella B. Buckley

We are always glad when April comes. Then we can find many flowers on our way to school. Even in February there are snowdrops in the orchard and Peter knows where he can sometimes find a primrose or violet in flower.

But we cannot get a good bunch until April. Before that the plants are busy growing their leaves.

The first bright flowers we find are daffodils in the fields, and the anemones in the woods. . . . They have very long, narrow leaves which come straight out of the ground. Each flower hangs on its own tall stalk. It has deep yellow tube in the middle, with a crown of pale yellow leaves round it.

Name _____ Date _____

Recycle It!

Ben's class learned about recycling. After school, Ben decided to convince his family to recycle.

"Dad, these glass bottles could be recycled and used again," said Ben. "These plastic cartons and cardboard boxes can too, Mom."

The next day, Ben and his family drove to the hardware store. They bought three big containers.

"Now we can all recycle our trash," instructed Ben. "The green container is for plastics. The red container is for glass. The yellow container is for paper and cardboard."

"I'll drive you to the recycling depot tomorrow," said Dad.

"Sounds good to me!" said Ben.

Name _____   Date _____

Ben's

Ben's class

Ben's class learned

Ben's class learned about

Ben's class learned about
recycling.

After

After school,

After school, Ben

After school, Ben decided

After school, Ben decided to

After school, Ben decided to
convince

After school, Ben decided to
convince his

After school, Ben decided to
convince his family

After school, Ben decided to
convince his family to

After school, Ben decided to
convince his family to recycle.

Recycle It!

Ben's class learned about recycling. After school, Ben decided to convince his family to recycle.

"Dad, these glass bottles could be recycled and used again," said Ben. "These plastic cartons and cardboard boxes can too, Mom."

The next day, Ben and his family drove to the hardware store. They bought three big containers.

"Now we can all recycle our trash," instructed Ben. "The green container is for plastics. The red container is for glass. The yellow container is for paper and cardboard."

"I'll drive you to the recycling depot tomorrow," said Dad.

"Sounds good to me!" said Ben.

Name _____   Date _____

Ben

too

used

after

boxes

Hardware store

Recycle It!

Ben's class learned about recycling. After school, Ben decided to convince his family to recycle.

"Dad, these glass bottles could be recycled and used again," said Ben. "These plastic cartons and cardboard boxes can too, Mom."

The next day, Ben and his family drove to the hardware store. They bought three big containers.

"Now we can all recycle our trash," instructed Ben. "The green container is for plastics. The red container is for glass. The yellow container is for paper and cardboard."

"I'll drive you to the recycling depot tomorrow," said Dad.

"Sounds good to me!" said Ben.

Name _____   Date _____

Song—The Owl
by Alfred Lord Tennyson

When cats run home and
light is come,

And dew is cold upon the
ground,

And the far-off stream is dumb,

And the whirring sail goes round,

And the whirring sail goes round;

Alone and warming his five wits,

The white owl in the belfry sits.

When merry milkmaids click the
latch,

And rarely smells the new-
mown hay,

And the cock hath sung beneath
the thatch

Twice or thrice his roundelay,

Twice or thrice his roundelay;

Alone and warming his five wits,

The white owl in the belfry sits.

Name _____   **Date** _____

When

When cats

When cats run

When cats run home

When cats run home and

When cats run home and
light

When cats run home and
light is

When cats run home and
light is come,

And

And dew

And dew is

And dew is cold

And dew is cold upon

And dew is cold upon the

And dew is cold upon the
ground,

Song—The Owl
by Alfred Lord Tennyson

When cats run home and
light is come,

And dew is cold upon the
ground,

And the far-off stream is dumb,

And the whirring sail goes round,

And the whirring sail goes round;

Alone and warming his five wits,

The white owl in the belfry sits.

When merry milkmaids click the
latch,

And rarely smells the new-
mown hay,

And the cock hath sung beneath
the thatch

Twice or thrice his roundelay,

Twice or thrice his roundelay;

Alone and warming his five wits,

The white owl in the belfry sits.

Name _____   Date _____

dew

run

owl

cats

cold

dumb

five

goes

home

sail

wits

white

belfry

far-off

ground

warming

whirring

Song—The Owl
by Alfred Lord Tennyson

When cats run home and
light is come,

And dew is cold upon the
ground,

And the far-off stream is dumb,

And the whirring sail goes round,

And the whirring sail goes round;

Alone and warming his five wits,

The white owl in the belfry sits.

When merry milkmaids click the
latch,

And rarely smells the new-
mown hay,

And the cock hath sung beneath
the thatch

Twice or thrice his roundelay,

Twice or thrice his roundelay;

Alone and warming his five wits,

The white owl in the belfry sits.

Name _____ Date _____

The Basketball Hoop

Michael and his dad always played basketball after school. One day the basketball hoop was broken.

"Someone must not want people to have fun," Michael complained.

Michael and his dad walked past the court the next morning. The hoop was missing. But it was back up after school.

"Look, the hoop is fixed. The person who fixed it must want people to have fun!" said Michael.

Mrs. Magee looked down from her window to the basketball court. She liked watching people have fun. That's why she had her son fix the hoop.

Name _____   Date _____

Michael

Michael and

Michael and his

Michael and his dad

Michael and his dad always

Michael and his dad always played

Michael and his dad always played basketball

Michael and his dad always played basketball after

Michael and his dad always played basketball after school.

One

One day

One day the

One day the basketball

One day the basketball hoop

One day the basketball hoop was

One day the basketball hoop was broken.

The Basketball Hoop

Michael and his dad always played basketball after school. One day the basketball hoop was broken.

"Someone must not want people to have fun," Michael complained.

Michael and his dad walked past the court the next morning. The hoop was missing. But it was back up after school.

"Look, the hoop is fixed. The person who fixed it must want people to have fun!" said Michael.

Mrs. Magee looked down from her window to the basketball court. She liked watching people have fun. That's why she had her son fix the hoop.

Name _____   Date _____

and

day

dad

his

one

the

was

back

hoop

after

always

broken

played

school

The Basketball Hoop

Michael and his dad always played basketball after school. One day the basketball hoop was broken.

"Someone must not want people to have fun," Michael complained.

Michael and his dad walked past the court the next morning. The hoop was missing. But it was back up after school.

"Look, the hoop is fixed. The person who fixed it must want people to have fun!" said Michael.

Mrs. Magee looked down from her window to the basketball court. She liked watching people have fun. That's why she had her son fix the hoop.

Name _____ Date _____

Global Alert

The cause of most air pollution is the burning of fuel. We burn fuel to heat buildings and run vehicles. We burn fuel to produce electricity. Burning fuel releases many substances that can pollute the air.

Refrigerators and air conditioners can cause pollution. So can the insulation that keeps our homes warm. Chemical substances from these appliances can leak into the atmosphere. Household items also release chemicals. They can cause harm to Earth's atmosphere. When foam products are burned, they release dangerous gases. These can include foam cups and plates from parties.

Name _____   Date _____

The

The cause

The cause of

The cause of most

The cause of most air

The cause of most air
pollution

The cause of most air
pollution is

The cause of most air
pollution is the

The cause of most air
pollution is the burning

The cause of most air
pollution is the burning of

The cause of most air
pollution is the burning of fuel.

Global Alert

The cause of most air pollution is the burning of fuel. We burn fuel to heat buildings and run vehicles. We burn fuel to produce electricity. Burning fuel releases many substances that can pollute the air.

Refrigerators and air conditioners can cause pollution. So can the insulation that keeps our homes warm. Chemical substances from these appliances can leak into the atmosphere. Household items also release chemicals. They can cause harm to Earth's atmosphere. When foam products are burned, they release dangerous gases. These can include foam cups and plates from parties.

Name _____   Date _____

is

of

air

run

the

burn

fuel

harm

heat

leak

many

most

produce

releases

pollution

Global Alert

The cause of most air pollution is the burning of fuel. We burn fuel to heat buildings and run vehicles. We burn fuel to produce electricity. Burning fuel releases many substances that can pollute the air.

Refrigerators and air conditioners can cause pollution. So can the insulation that keeps our homes warm. Chemical substances from these appliances can leak into the atmosphere. Household items also release chemicals. They can cause harm to Earth's atmosphere. When foam products are burned, they release dangerous gases. These can include foam cups and plates from parties.

Name _____ Date _____

The Farmer and His Sons

an Aesop's Fable, retold by Milo Winter

A rich old farmer called his sons to his bedside.

"My sons," he said, "heed what I have to say. Somewhere on our farm is hidden a rich treasure. I do not know the exact spot, but it is there."

The sons set to work digging with all their might, turning up every foot of ground with their spades, and going over the whole farm two or three times.

They found no gold, but at harvest time they had a profit far greater than their neighbors. It was then that they understood that the treasure their father told them about was the wealth of a bountiful crop, and that in their industry had they found the treasure.

Industry is itself a treasure.

Name _____ **Date** _____

A

A rich

A rich old

A rich old farmer,

A rich old farmer called

A rich old farmer called his

A rich old farmer called his sons

A rich old farmer called his sons to

A rich old farmer called his sons to his

A rich old farmer called his sons to his bedside.

The Farmer and His Sons
an Aesop's Fable, retold by Milo Winter

A rich old farmer called his sons to his bedside.

"My sons," he said, "heed what I have to say. Somewhere on our farm is hidden a rich treasure. I do not know the exact spot, but it is there."

The sons set to work digging with all their might, turning up every foot of ground with their spades, and going over the whole farm two or three times.

They found no gold, but at harvest time they had a profit far greater than their neighbors. It was then that they understood that the treasure their father told them about was the wealth of a bountiful crop, and that in their industry had they found the treasure.

Industry is itself a treasure.

Name _____ Date _____

to

his

old

say

days

felt

have

heed

rich

said

sons

what

called

farmer

bedside

The Farmer and His Sons
an Aesop's Fable, retold by Milo Winter

A rich old farmer called his sons to his bedside.

"My sons," he said, "heed what I have to say. Somewhere on our farm is hidden a rich treasure. I do not know the exact spot, but it is there."

The sons set to work digging with all their might, turning up every foot of ground with their spades, and going over the whole farm two or three times.

They found no gold, but at harvest time they had a profit far greater than their neighbors. It was then that they understood that the treasure their father told them about was the wealth of a bountiful crop, and that in their industry had they found the treasure.

Industry is itself a treasure.

Name _____ Date _____

excerpt from
"How the Leaves Came Down"
by Susan Coolidge

I'll tell you how the leaves came down.

   The great Tree to his children said,

  "You're getting sleepy, Yellow and Brown,

   Yes, very sleepy, little Red;

   It is quite time to go to bed."

"Ah!" begged each silly, pouting leaf,

  "Let us a little longer stay;

Dear Father Tree, behold our grief,

  'Tis such a very pleasant day

We do not want to go away."

So, just for one more merry day

  To the great Tree the leaflets clung,

Frolicked and danced and had their way,

  Upon the autumn breezes swung,

  Whispering all their sports among—

"Perhaps the great Tree will forget

  And let us stay until the spring

If we all beg and coax and fret."

Name _____   Date _____

I'll

I'll tell

I'll tell you

I'll tell you how

I'll tell you how the

I'll tell you how the leaves

I'll tell you how the leaves came

I'll tell you how the leaves came down.

The

The great

The great Tree

The great Tree to

The great Tree to his

The great Tree to his children

The great Tree to his children said,

excerpt from
"How the Leaves Came Down"
by Susan Coolidge

I'll tell you how the leaves came down.

   The great Tree to his children said,

 "You're getting sleepy, Yellow and Brown,

   Yes, very sleepy, little Red;

   It is quite time to go to bed."

"Ah!" begged each silly, pouting leaf,

   "Let us a little longer stay;

Dear Father Tree, behold our grief,

   'Tis such a very pleasant day

We do not want to go away."

So, just for one more merry day

   To the great Tree the leaflets clung,

Frolicked and danced and had their way,

   Upon the autumn breezes swung,

   Whispering all their sports among—

"Perhaps the great Tree will forget

   And let us stay until the spring

If we all beg and coax and fret."

Name _____   Date _____

bed

how

stay

tell

tree

want

clung

grief

quite

silly

begged

behold

sleepy

pouting

pleasant

excerpt from
"How the Leaves Came Down"

by Susan Coolidge

I'll tell you how the leaves came down.

   The great Tree to his children said,

  "You're getting sleepy, Yellow and Brown,

    Yes, very sleepy, little Red;

    It is quite time to go to bed."

"Ah!" begged each silly, pouting leaf,

   "Let us a little longer stay;

Dear Father Tree, behold our grief,

   'Tis such a very pleasant day

We do not want to go away."

So, just for one more merry day

   To the great Tree the leaflets clung,

Frolicked and danced and had their way,

    Upon the autumn breezes swung,

    Whispering all their sports among—

"Perhaps the great Tree will forget

   And let us stay until the spring

If we all beg and coax and fret."

Name _____ Date _____

The Missing Rabbit

Tom's floppy-eared rabbit escaped from her cage.

"She can't go anywhere, Tom," said Dad. "The yard is completely fenced in."

Tom looked everywhere. But with so many trees and bushes, he couldn't find Thumper.

Night came and still there was no sign of Thumper. "Let's put out some carrots," said Tom. "Maybe that will make her come home."

They placed carrots throughout the yard. Later, Tom when to see if Thumper had come home.

"The carrots are gone, and there's Thumper!" shouted Tom, pointing toward the cage. "I'm glad she eats carrots, because they must have helped her find her way home in the dark!"

Name _____   Date _____

Tom's

Tom's floppy-eared

Tom's floppy-eared rabbit

Tom's floppy-eared rabbit escaped

Tom's floppy-eared rabbit escaped from

Tom's floppy-eared rabbit escaped from her

Tom's floppy-eared rabbit escaped from her cage.

"She

"She can't

"She can't go

"She can't go anywhere,

"She can't go anywhere, Tom,"

"She can't go anywhere, Tom," said

"She can't go anywhere, Tom," said Dad.

The Missing Rabbit

Tom's floppy-eared rabbit escaped from her cage.

"She can't go anywhere, Tom," said Dad. "The yard is completely fenced in."

Tom looked everywhere. But with so many trees and bushes, he couldn't find Thumper.

Night came and still there was no sign of Thumper. "Let's put out some carrots," said Tom. "Maybe that will make her come home."

They placed carrots throughout the yard. Later, Tom when to see if Thumper had come home.

"The carrots are gone, and there's Thumper!" shouted Tom, pointing toward the cage. "I'm glad she eats carrots, because they must have helped her find her way home in the dark!"

Name _____ **Date** _____

go

is

Dad

her

Tom

cage

can't

yard

fenced

rabbit

escaped

completely

floppy-eared

The Missing Rabbit

Tom's floppy-eared rabbit escaped from her cage.

"She can't go anywhere, Tom," said Dad. "The yard is completely fenced in."

Tom looked everywhere. But with so many trees and bushes, he couldn't find Thumper.

Night came and still there was no sign of Thumper. "Let's put out some carrots," said Tom. "Maybe that will make her come home."

They placed carrots throughout the yard. Later, Tom when to see if Thumper had come home.

"The carrots are gone, and there's Thumper!" shouted Tom, pointing toward the cage. "I'm glad she eats carrots, because they must have helped her find her way home in the dark!"

Name _____ Date _____

Math to Munch

The label on a food package gives the weight of the package's contents. The weight is usually given in both ounces and grams. Ounces are the unit of weight used in the United Sates, while grams are the unit of weight used in other countries. A slice of bread usually weighs around one ounce, or 28 grams.

Food packages also have other numbers listed in a table called Nutrition Facts. These numbers give such information as the amount of fat or protein found in the food.

The Nutrition Facts table also gives the number of calories per serving of food. Calories are units used to measure the amount of energy in food. Your body needs a certain amount of energy—and, therefore, calories—each day. The more active you are, the more calories you need.

Name _____ Date _____

The

The label

The label on

The label on a

The label on a food

The label on a food
package

The label on a food
package gives

The label on a food
package gives the

The label on a food
package gives the weight

The label on a food
package gives the weight
of

The label on a food
package gives the weight
of the

The label on a food
package gives the weight
of the package's

The label on a food
package gives the weight
of the package's contents.

Math to Munch

The label on a food package gives the weight of the package's contents. The weight is usually given in both ounces and grams. Ounces are the unit of weight used in the United Sates, while grams are the unit of weight used in other countries. A slice of bread usually weighs around one ounce, or 28 grams.

Food packages also have other numbers listed in a table called Nutrition Facts. These numbers give such information as the amount of fat or protein found in the food.

The Nutrition Facts table also gives the number of calories per serving of food. Calories are units used to measure the amount of energy in food. Your body needs a certain amount of energy—and, therefore, calories—each day. The more active you are, the more calories you need.

Name _____   Date _____

is

of

you

both

food

unit

used

gives

grams

label

ounces

weight

package

countries

Math to Munch

The label on a food package gives the weight of the package's contents. The weight is usually given in both ounces and grams. Ounces are the unit of weight used in the United Sates, while grams are the unit of weight used in other countries. A slice of bread usually weighs around one ounce, or 28 grams.

Food packages also have other numbers listed in a table called Nutrition Facts. These numbers give such information as the amount of fat or protein found in the food.

The Nutrition Facts table also gives the number of calories per serving of food. Calories are units used to measure the amount of energy in food. Your body needs a certain amount of energy—and, therefore, calories—each day. The more active you are, the more calories you need.

Name _____ Date _____

Colonial Times

During colonial times, people
believed in the importance of hard
work. They believed that it was
terribly wrong to be lazy.

Even so, colonial people took time
to have fun. They shared meals with
family and friends. They celebrated
such events as holidays, weddings,
harvests, and the construction of a
home or barn.

Colonial children worked hard,
too, but they also found ways to
have fun. Boys climbed trees, made
and flew kites, and played with
leather balls filled with feathers.
And they enjoyed carving objects
out of wood with pocketknives. Girls
played mostly with dolls that they
made from rags or from cornhusks
(the leaves that cover an ear of
corn). Children also sang songs,
rolled hoops, rode horseback, and
played such games as tag, hide-
and-seek, and charades.

Name _____ Date _____

During

During colonial

During colonial times,

During colonial times, people

During colonial times, people believed

During colonial times, people believed in

During colonial times, people believed in the

During colonial times, people believed in the importance

During colonial times, people believed in the importance of

During colonial times, people believed in the importance of hard

During colonial times, people believed in the importance of hard work.

Colonial Times

During colonial times, people believed in the importance of hard work. They believed that it was terribly wrong to be lazy.

Even so, colonial people took time to have fun. They shared meals with family and friends. They celebrated such events as holidays, weddings, harvests, and the construction of a home or barn.

Colonial children worked hard, too, but they also found ways to have fun. Boys climbed trees, made and flew kites, and played with leather balls filled with feathers. And they enjoyed carving objects out of wood with pocketknives. Girls played mostly with dolls that they made from rags or from cornhusks (the leaves that cover an ear of corn). Children also sang songs, rolled hoops, rode horseback, and played such games as tag, hide-and-seek, and charades.

Name _____   Date _____

be

in

was

hard

lazy

that

work

wrong

people

believed

colonial

terribly

importance

Colonial Times

During colonial times, people believed in the importance of hard work. They believed that it was terribly wrong to be lazy.

Even so, colonial people took time to have fun. They shared meals with family and friends. They celebrated such events as holidays, weddings, harvests, and the construction of a home or barn.

Colonial children worked hard, too, but they also found ways to have fun. Boys climbed trees, made and flew kites, and played with leather balls filled with feathers. And they enjoyed carving objects out of wood with pocketknives. Girls played mostly with dolls that they made from rags or from cornhusks (the leaves that cover an ear of corn). Children also sang songs, rolled hoops, rode horseback, and played such games as tag, hide-and-seek, and charades.

Recording Time Sheet

Student Name: _____

Date: _____

1st Reading: _____

2nd Reading: _____

3rd Reading: _____

To calculate the student's accuracy percentage:

– Count the total number of words in the reading passage.

– Count the total number of errors.

– Subtract the number of errors from the total number of words. This is the number of words the student read correctly.

– To calculate the student's accuracy percentage, divide the number of student's correct words by the total number of words in the passage. Then multiply this number by 100.

Example:
Passage: 70 words
Student Errors: 5
Words Correct (WC): 65
Accuracy Percentage Rate: 65/70 = 92% accuracy

Comprehension Monitoring

To monitor student's comprehension of texts, ask the following questions:

For Literary Texts (fiction/poetry/drama)

- In your own words, what is this [story/poem/play] about?

- Who is/are the character(s) in this [story/poem/play]?

- Where does the [story/poem/play] take place? When does it take place?

- Are there illustrations in the [story/poem/play]? How do they help you better understand the story?

- What is/are the character(s) doing? Describe their actions.

- Is there a problem the character(s) need to solve? How do they solve it?

- How and why do the characters change over the course of the story?

- Do you think the things that happen in this [story/poem/play] are true?

- What happened at the beginning, middle, and end of the [story/poem/play]?

For Informational Texts

- What is this text about?

- Recall two important facts or details. Why are they important?

- Explain in your own words what the author is saying about _____.

- What idea does the author present first? What does the author tell us next?

- What do you think the author wants you to learn from reading this text?

- How well do you think the author conveys the information? Is the author biased?

- What photos, maps, tables, or diagrams are included? How do they help you better understand the information?

- How does _____ relate to _____?

My Fluency Self-Evaluation

Text I just read: _____

Accuracy Did I read the words correctly?	
Rate/Pace Did I read at the right speed for the text?	
Intonation and Expression Did I read with feeling and variety to engage the listeners?	
Understanding Did I read in a way that indicated that I understood the words I was reading?	

Check off one goal you want to work on:

_____ Read more accurately;

_____ Read more quickly;

_____ Read more slowly;

_____ Read with more expression.